947
FRO

BAR014099

P9-DML-864

OBSOLETE - OK TO DONATE
DATE:

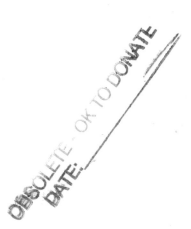

TITLE 1
IASA PL103 - 382

BARBOUR SCHOOL LIBRARY
ROCKFORD, ILLINOIS

A Look at Russia

by Helen Frost

Consulting Editor: Gail Saunders-Smith, Ph.D.

Consultant: Nancy Shields Kollmann, Ph.D.
Professor of Russian History
Stanford University

Pebble Books

an imprint of Capstone Press
Mankato, Minnesota

Pebble Books are published by Capstone Press
151 Good Counsel Drive, P.O. Box 669, Mankato, Minnesota 56002
http://www.capstone-press.com

Copyright © 2002 Capstone Press. All rights reserved.
No part of this publication may be reproduced in whole or in part, or stored in a
retrieval system, or transmitted in any form or by any means, electronic, mechanical,
photocopying, recording, or otherwise, without written permission of the publisher.
For information regarding permission, write to Capstone Press,
151 Good Counsel Drive, P.O. Box 669, Dept. R, Mankato, Minnesota 56002.
Printed in the United States of America.

2 3 4 5 6 07 06 05 04 03 02

Library of Congress Cataloging-in-Publication Data
Frost, Helen, 1949–
    A look at Russia / by Helen Frost.
    p. cm.—(Our world)
    Includes bibliographical references and index.
    ISBN 0-7368-0986-4 (hardcover)
    ISBN 0-7368-9424-1 (paperback)
    1. Russia (Federation)—Social life and customs—Juvenile literature.
    2. Russia (Federation)—Environmental conditions—Juvenile literature.
    [1. Russia (Federation)] I. Title. II. Series: Our world (Pebble Books)
DK510.32 .F76 2002
947—dc21   00-012927

Summary: Simple text and photographs depict the land, animals, and people
of Russia.

Note to Parents and Teachers

The Our World series supports national social studies standards
related to culture. This book describes and illustrates the land,
animals, and people of Russia. The photographs support early
readers in understanding the text. The repetition of words and
phrases helps early readers learn new words. This book also
introduces early readers to subject-specific vocabulary words, which
are defined in the Words to Know section. Early readers may need
assistance to read some words and to use the Table of Contents,
Words to Know, Read More, Internet Sites, and Index/Word List
sections of the book.

Table of Contents

★ Moscow

Russia

Russia is the largest country in the world. Russia covers parts of Europe and northern Asia. The capital of Russia is Moscow.

Russia's flag

Most of Russia has
long, cold winters.
Southern Russia has
milder weather. Russia
has forests, mountains,
tundra, and plains.

reindeer

Siberian tiger

Reindeer live on the tundra and in forests. Siberian tigers live on Russia's mountains.

About 150 million people live in Russia. They speak Russian. They use the Cyrillic alphabet to write the Russian language.

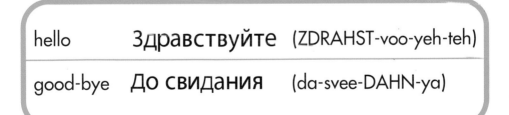

hello	Здравствуйте	(ZDRAHST-voo-yeh-teh)
good-bye	До свидания	(da-svee-DAHN-ya)

Russians eat meat, cheese, and bread. They make soup with beets, potatoes, and cabbage.

Many Russians play chess.
Ice hockey and soccer
are popular sports in Russia.
Many Russians enjoy dancing
and gymnastics.

Some Russians fish to earn money. Many Russians work in factories. Some Russians own stores and restaurants.

Russia's money is counted in rubles.

Many Russians travel
on trains and planes.
They also ride subways
and buses in cities.

Lake Baikal is in Russia. It is the deepest freshwater lake in the world. It holds one-fifth of the world's freshwater.

Words to Know

Cyrillic—the Russian alphabet; the Cyrillic alphabet has 33 letters.

freshwater—water that does not have salt

language—the words and grammar that people use to talk and write to each other; many languages are spoken in Russia; the Russian language is the official language of Russia.

Moscow—the capital city of Russia; about 9 million people live in Moscow.

reindeer—a type of deer that lives in the world's far northern regions

Siberian tiger—a kind of tiger that lives in Siberia; Siberia is a region in eastern Russia.

subway—a system of trains that runs underground in a city

tundra—a large plain that remains frozen most of the year; no trees grow on the tundra.

Read More

Conboy, Fiona, and Terence M. G. Rice. *Welcome to Russia.* Welcome to My Country. Milwaukee: Gareth Stevens, 2000.

Nickles, Greg. *Russia: The Land.* Lands, Peoples and Cultures Series. New York: Crabtree, 2000.

Schemenauer, Elma. *Russia.* Faces and Places. Chanhassen, Minn.: Child's World, 1999.

Thoennes, Kristin. *Russia.* Countries of the World. Mankato, Minn.: Bridgestone Books, 1999.

Internet Sites

The Official Guide to Russia
http://www.interknowledge.com/russia

Russia Geography 2000
http://www.photius.com/wfb2000/countries/russia/russia_geography.html

Index/Word List

Word Count: 161
Early-Intervention Level: 17

Editorial Credits
Mari C. Schuh, editor; Kia Bielke, cover designer and illustrator; Kimberly Danger,
   photo researcher

Photo Credits
International Stock/Ellen Rooney, 1
Mike Yamashita/Woodfin Camp and Associates, 18
Photri-Microstock, 14, 20
Stephen G. Donaldson Photography, 12
Visuals Unlimited/Jeff Greenberg, cover, 10, 16; Ernest Manewal, 6 (top); Charles
   McRae, 6 (bottom); Tom Walker, 8 (top); Joe McDonald, 8 (bottom)

The author thanks the children's section staff at the Allen County Public Library in
Fort Wayne, Indiana, for research assistance.